How to Join
a Sorority

Tips, Tricks, and Advice
for Sorority Rush
and Making the Cut

by Macy Anderson

Table of Contents

Introduction

Having been on the Rush Committee of my Sorority multiple years, I can tell you the what, why, and how of joining a Sorority. And not just your run of the mill female organization at that, but rather, I'll focus on how to get in to some of the more prestigious sororities with the most grueling application process.

At the get go, you need to be selective on what Sorority you will apply for. This is because some of the more prestigious sororities have a rule of not accepting applicants who have already been a member of another Sorority. The rationale is simple; this prevents bad blood between sororities and upholds a certain degree of exclusivity. In other words, pride and the rule book will not allow a Sorority to take the leftovers or quitters from other sororities, rivals or not.

Another reason that should put you on high alert is the fact that, once you've quit or have been rejected by a Sorority, although you may technically be allowed to re-apply, the chances of being accepted are slim to none. That is why it is important to be prepared in terms of researching enough about all the Sorority options that you have a good idea which one(s) you would be interested in joining and being a member of for the long haul. This book will show you how.

Thanks again for purchasing this book, I hope you enjoy it!

Chapter 1: What is a Sorority?

Sorority comes from the Latin root word "Soror," meaning sister. A Sorority is usually named using Greek words i.e. Alpha Rho Talionis. The same then uses the acronym for easy identification i.e. ART. However, this is not an absolute rule because some well known sororities use English words. Also, some sororities are better known for their "nicknames." This is usually derived from their formal names. For example: Zeta Tau Alpha maybe better known as just Zeta; Kappa Delta, as KD.

Logically speaking, the membership consists of all female members. In other words, membership is first and foremost, gender based although there are sororities known to have ties with 1 specific fraternity (i.e., their 'brother' fraternity). These are usually undergraduate societies, and most of the top sororities provide their members with perks, i.e. Sorority house, invitations to exclusive social events, friends, employment introductions, a social network that lasts beyond graduation, etc.

A Sorority has the same code of camaraderie as most organizations. However, true sororities are a cut above simple organizations because of the level of dedication required to apply, serve as a 'pledge', and become a full fledged member. This can be anywhere from a week, month, or even several months. Some sororities require an applicant, also known as a rushee, pledge, initiate, etc. to apply for membership while other sororities are strictly by invitation only. Most colleges and universities these days have a formal system by which girls can 'rush' many sororities at the same time, and while the girls whittle down their choices for sororities, the sororities are whittling down their choices for new members at the same time.

As a general rule, a "rushee" is a female applicant to a Sorority who has not yet passed the first phase of application, nor has she been given any invitation. After the Sorority rush, sororities invite or bid on viable applicants who then become a pledge or initiate. If the pledge passes and completes a specific period of time and certain requirements, then she becomes elevated to the level of initiate, and there is often a ceremony that accompanies this. Realistically speaking, form phase one to phase 2, the process is more of getting to know other Sorority members, and showing your personality and skill set to them so they know you would be a valuable asset to their organization. On the third phase, if you get accepted as an initiate, then come the secret rituals, the possibility of living in the house, and pretty much full access to all the organization is and has to offer.

Hazing is illegal in most jurisdictions and in 44 states here in the US, and Sorority hazing is not nearly as common as in Fraternities. For the most part, the more prestigious Sororities treat their new pledges very well, giving them gifts and taking them out to dinner, etc., whereas Fraternities are more likely to engage in hazing and making their new pledges do crazy or embarrassing things, or perform manual labor or run errands for the brothers of the fraternity. However, of course due to the secretive nature of a Sorority, hazing is occasionally a reality and is said to be under-reported. And yes, physical abuse although unlikely is a possibility. If you are in a situation of being hazed, and you don't think it's just silly or funny but rather it's actually making you feel uncomfortable, then speak up and get yourself out of the situation. No Sorority is worth losing your sense of self-esteem or your sense of right and wrong.

Strictly speaking, a Sorority has to meet certain requirements in order to validly exist. For example, most sororities are required to apply for recognition in its home university. This also means that the Sorority has to comply with regulations and willingly undergo supervision by school authorities. The most obvious of which involves the final stage of the initiation in which the school has to be informed of when, where and who will be involved.

In fact, there is a list of sororities in most jurisdictions. They are usually subdivided into national chapters, sub organizations, school or profession based etc. I encourage all applicants to look for the Sorority in a national database. This ensures that you are joining a legitimate organization. This will also aid you in determining how prestigious the organization is.

Realistically speaking though, a Sorority is steeped in secrecy. As such, much of the actual "rites" performed are a closely guarded secret. You may hear snippets of what goes on, but even then these are mere gossip, and incomplete information.

Chapter 2: Sorority Rush

The word "Rush" refers to the rush in recruitment and application (and excitement!). It usually involves the grueling process of going from Sorority house to Sorority house, meeting and being interviewed by multiple Sorority sisters, and also watching the sisters perform skits, sing, and dance. Think of it similar to a job interview, keeping in mind that you are not only selling yourself as a valuable asset to the Sorority, but they are also selling themselves as a valuable organization worth joining. As a "rushee," you should expect and be prepared for sharing something personal about yourself, etc. They want to get to know you, and know more about your hobbies, interests, skills, and talent sets. If you sang in the church choir, this is the time to let them know. The goal is for you to highlight what you can offer. If you make a good impression then you will get an invitation for the next cut.

Depending on the status of the Sorority as well as the total student body, a rush can be a formal event with you wearing a dress and family jewelry, attending a tea party or dressing casually. Usually your school will give you some sort of guide or schedule explaining what to wear on the various days of rush. For example, maybe they'll suggest you dress casually on Day 1, and progressively more formal until you're suggested to wear a little black cocktail dress on Day 5.

I advise you to take your time, and although you may have followed my advice to do research on each Sorority before the rush process begins, really be open-minded and get to know each Sorority as you experience it during rush. No need to jump into an early decision with the first Sorority that gives you a smile. Remember, a Sorority maybe most visible and demanding during a specific period of time, especially during your college years. But you will belong to the organization far longer than that. Choosing the right Sorority can even mean an easier time applying for a job or acquiring a professional social sphere. Take your time, make a good impression on all of them, as if each one was your top choice for the short period of time you visit during rush. Don't blow any of them off quite yet. Stay engaged, and keep all your options open until you reach the deadline to make a decision.

Endorsement Letter

If you know someone within the Sorority, or if you know someone who is a recent graduate or alumna of a Sorority, this is a big advantage. Ask that person to write an endorsement letter on your behalf. If you know someone who is of high standing in the community, ask for a general endorsement letter. This is especially true of it is someone the Sorority holds in high esteem, such as a distinguished alumni.

If you have high academic or sports potential, ask your class advisor or coach for an endorsement letter. These letters of recommendation are sometimes required during a Sorority rush. But even if not, it helps you stand out from other applicants, and these letters are certainly considered when the sisters are making their final decisions.

Tip: if you have a Sorority in mind in advance, but don't know anyone to write an endorsement letter for you, then find out where an alumni might be near you. Try to get in as a temp, trainee or summer intern. Now impress that alumni with your performance. Don't be needy and ask for a referral letter outright. Be subtle about it! Mention in passing that you got into so and so university and you want to major in such and such. If you make a good impression, you won't even have to ask for the referral letter, because the alumni will volunteer to write it for you. Worst comes to worst, suck it up and ask for that letter on your last day. If nothing else, you at least have something or someone in common to talk about with the Sorority during rush!

Chapter 3: Key Tips During Rush

First Impressions Count

Whatever type of Sorority you want to join in, you want to be at your absolute best. The first rule of thumb is to be yourself. Yup, cliché as it may sound, trying to be someone you are not will only result in a bad match. It's like trying to fit into a dress 1 size smaller. While you can probably squeeze into it for a good couple of minutes, or even a couple of hours, you aren't going to be comfortable the whole time! You'll end up with a better match if you focus on just being comfortable in your own skin, even if it doesn't seem to gel with a particular Sorority, or the person you're being interviewed by during rush at a particular Sorority.

Be approachable. Wear something fit for the occasion. If it is orientation day, go for something comfortable and flattering. This ensures that you catch the eye of recruiters for the right reason. Don't be the girl who goes to check your mail at the campus mailbox in your pajamas. Yes, it's college, and you're on your own and want to be comfortable, but you never know who else you may run into, and if a Sorority sister sees you out somewhere looking shabby, it will likely get back to the rest of the sisters.

Getting a good night's sleep and eating a healthy breakfast before your day of Rush starts is critical. Some Sorority rushes can last the whole day with very little time to eat. Bring with you a non-messy snack i.e. banana, small pack of cashews, a bottle of water, etc. The last thing you want is to faint or not be able to concentrate to the person you're speaking with because you're starving.

Tip: upper class Sorority members will be friendly and approachable during orientation day. They will laugh with you and be very accommodating. But make no mistake, if you rub them the wrong way, they will remember your face and name. As a general rule, if one member feels strongly about saying no, then regardless of your performance and endorsement letter, you are out.

Here are some key tips during Rush:

1. Don't wear flashy jewelry or skimpy outfits

2. Avoid bragging about your accomplishments

3. Don't tell them about the time you blacked out in a party!

4. Keep your eyes off the boys. You never know if a Sorority member has dibs!

5. Never talk down to or belittle the accomplishments of the Sorority.

6. Avoid uncomfortable high heels. You will be on your feet a lot during Rush, and you may even have to walk several blocks to go from one Sorority house to another. Better be comfy.

7. Bring a few feminine essentials like loose powder, oil blotting face pad, a little mirror, lip gloss, feminine pad or tampon, etc. Basically, anything you need for a quick fix.

8. Don't forget to apply some deodorant and carry mints with you!

9. Bring your resume just in case, keep it folded neatly in your purse.

Body Language

When talking with other Sorority members during rush, you need to be open and accommodating both in the words you choose and your body language. Avoid crossing your legs and arms, although if you're wearing a skirt or dress you should cross your ankles in a lady-like manner. Occasionally look into the eyes of the person you are talking to, and try to make sure your face is conveying at least a hint of a smile at all times, unless for some reason you're discussing a serious topic. Avoid any barriers. Always talk to the person with your body facing them. Really listen to what they are saying or asking, and nod at the appropriate time to demonstrate you've heard them. All of these little things add up as indicators that you are intently listening and are open to the possibility of membership and friendship.

Ask Questions

Don't just nod your head and agree. Ask appropriate questions, and then follow up with your own thoughts on the matter. I suggest that if you have a particular Sorority in mind, you should read up on it in advance. This way you can steer the conversation into flattering information for the Sorority, which will in turn score positive points for you. Don't be a kiss ass though. As a general rule of thumb, mix it up with

2 parts researched flattery and 1 part skepticism. Just make sure to leave wiggle room for them to easily contest your last statement. For example, you can tell them how you've heard they won Greek Week last year, and how they dominated at the School's dance-off contest the year before that. But then for the 'skepticism' part, maybe explain how it's important to you to find a Sorority where you can express your singing talents. That leaves room for the sister you're talking with to then say "Oh, well let me tell you about our Sorority Choir events and Sing-a-Thons. You absolutely must meet Melissa, she's such a great singer and is even planning on trying out for American Idol this year!" Thus, you've found a way to express your talent as a singer, and also allowed the sister to give you reassurance that you do indeed fit in to their Sorority. She's even excited now to introduce you to her Sorority sister Melissa. This subconsciously will put her on your side when the decision making process begins – you now have an inner-ally!

Tip: most sororities have a website. Browse the same. Check out their Facebook group to see who's who in the alumni pool. Look for common ground or a mutually interesting topic that you can talk about.

Here's another example of the two flatteries plus one skepticism mix: "I heard, one of your alumni just got that new marketing position at coca-cola, congratulations. Have you met her by any chance?" Follow up with, "Wow, your track record of top students is impressive!" Now add to the mix, "but I heard, you're a little extreme when it comes to the screening and service of your initiates..." That last question provides an opportunity for the member to brag about how their tough screening process is not for everyone, and that it produces positive results, as evidenced by the first two statements you just made.

That's a win for you! Psychology 101: If you want someone to connect with you, then make them want to please you or allow them to win an argument with you. This makes them feel that they've invested in you, so might as well keep you!

Of course you want to ask questions that you truly want the answers to, for your own information and benefit. Here are important topics to ask about that will give you more insight about the Sorority:

- Academic programs (Sorority's average GPA, Study or Tutoring Programs or Buddies, etc.)

- Community involvement (Charity Events, Social Events, etc.)

- Sorority housing (How many people get to live in the house at the same time? How much does it cost? How many girls per room? Etc.)

- Minimum and maximum time commitment (Are you required to attend all the social events? How frequent and how long are the chapter meetings? What other obligations will you have as far as how much time you must be available on a weekly basis?)

- What kinds of qualities are they looking for in new members?

Don't Approach It with an Attitude of "What Can You Offer Me?"

Of course this is at the back of your mind. But come rush time you want to instead come across as "This is what I can offer you!" Highlight your achievements, strengths, assets, skills. Be friendly and upbeat. Talk about different things you've done for your community in the past, and how passionate you are about that. Speak with confidence, but not with arrogance, being careful not to come across as bragging. Also, be calm and relaxed, don't sound panicked, rushed, or psychotic. It is a stressful time, and minutes fly by quickly and you have so much to say, but being cool, calm, and collected goes a long way in showing them that you are an emotionally mature person.

Chapter 4: Understanding It's a Numbers Game

Think of a Sorority rush as a miniaturized version of America's Got Talent. You line up outside, wait for your turn on the stage, and you've got a few minutes to make your mark. And this is the best case scenario. Realistically speaking, if a Sorority house processes a couple of hundred rushees in a single day, then you need to make a good impression to make the cut.

This is probably why some outsiders have a tendency to dismiss the rush as useless because they believe most sororities assess you on physical appearance only. This just is not the case. Sororities are looking to build their organization and reputation, and they need to find people with a variety of skills and talents. The best sororities typically want athletes, singers, dancers, academics, etc., the list goes on and on. They want to be the "best" in every category, sort of like a well-rounded dream team. So what if you're not "really, really, really ridiculously good looking" (quoting the movie Zoolander here). Who cares? What are you good at that isn't skin deep? The key really is to be able to express this to the Sorority members in the short amount of time you have to speak with them. For example, if you're a star soccer player in high school, don't neglect to mention that (in a non-bragging, modest way of course) before you leave that Sorority house!

Think of it this way. If you were given 3 minutes to make an impression, how will you go about doing so? Plan that 3 minutes to in advance!

5 Questions You Will Be Asked

Make sure you have prepared suitable responses to these 5 important questions. Keep things short and simple, and again, find a way to express your answers without sounding arrogant. (There's nothing worse than a prospective pledge who's full of herself!). You want to be specific and encourage the organizer to ask you follow up questions.

1. What are your academic and non academic achievements?

2. Why do you want to join our Sorority? (The best answer is along the lines of "to serve and to grow", of course expressed in a more specific way)

3. What unique attributes can you bring to the table?

4. Who are your role models?

5. What are your strengths and your weaknesses?

Tip: Don't be vague. And never try to pass off a weakness as a strength. For example: I am so detail oriented that I sometimes fail to meet deadlines. This is you finding an excuse for a weakness. Own up to your weakness but then you can explain what you're doing to overcome it. For example, say that sometimes you don't meet deadlines, but you are working to overcome your weakness by downloading a journal app to keep you more organized.

Prioritize Your First Choice

Often times, your College or University will set up your Rush schedule for you, and you just have to go to the house on the schedule during the specified time. However, if you happen to be a college that allows you to schedule your own rush, then definitely go to your preferred Sorority house first. Then, pick a lesser known Sorority house second, or one that you are less enthusiastic about based on your initial research. Rotate among your top picks and your back up picks. This way you have a better chance of getting an invitation. In any case, keep an open mind. So many times I've heard of girls who thought they wanted to join a certain Sorority, until they got to know a different one better during rush. Staying positive and open minded, and being friendly with all of the sororities you visit will keep your options open for you to make a decision in the future.

Realize You May Not Be Chosen by Your First Choice

Again, this is all a numbers game. So you are rushing with hundreds of other girls, right? And let's say each Sorority can only take in 30 new members. Well, if you are number 32 or 33 on your favorite Sorority's list at the end of it all, then you didn't make it. Don't be discouraged or upset. By keeping an open mind and getting to know all the sororities you've visited, most likely you realize by now there are several great choices. Maybe it's just meant to be with your Second Choice, and great things will happen between you and this organization that you never could have imagined. Instead of spending Bid Day being upset you didn't get picked by your first choice, just go greet your new sisters at the Sorority that did accept you with open arms and a huge smile.

Chapter 5: Do Your Research and Be Honest

Some schools will require you to go thru the entire Sorority row. Other schools allow you to choose which Sorority to rush for. Some sororities only entertain those who have endorsement letters. Some sororities will hold a talent contest. Simply put, there are different rules when it comes to applying for admittance to a Sorority. Knowing the rules will make sure you don't embarrass yourself and end up on the black list.

Do Your Research

This cannot be over emphasized! I have heard of stories where a rushee goes to a Sorority house thinking it is another. Worst, the same rushee goes about maligning the "rival Sorority" not knowing the she is standing in that same Sorority house! There are also instances a rushee tries to drum up the conversation by congratulating a Sorority for something they did not participate in. As mentioned earlier, go online. Read the literature. Grab flyers during orientation day. Be informed.

In some cases, you need to sign up for recruitment day. It's best to do this early on. This is because, in some cases, there are limited slots. Tip: recruitment day is usually posted on the college's website. At the very least ask the person orienting you around campus about last year's recruitment day. In my case, little did I know that the guy who was assigned by my freshman dorm to show all of us newbies around campus was actually the boyfriend of one of my future Sorority sisters. So weeks before rush began, he had already given my name to his girlfriend and told her all about me, long before I walked in that Sorority house door. So keep in mind to be at your best from the moment you set foot on campus, because sometimes you're already being assessed by someone who knows one of the Sorority sisters.

Be Honest

You will have to fill out an application letter and/or submit some sort of resume. Be honest with your declarations. Dishonesty will always come out in the long run, whether next week or next year.

Chapter 6: How Sisters Decide Who Makes the Cut

Different Sororities have different procedures in determining who makes the cut. However, as a rushee, having some idea of how it all works will help you understand the importance of the impression you make with the sisters you meet during Rush. Also, as I mentioned earlier, the good impressions you leave on people need to extend beyond rush and beyond Sorority sisters – you never know who on campus might know one of the sisters, and everything you do is open to leaving an impression that can get passed along in no time like wild fire. Be smart about it.

So, from your perspective, you've gone to a bunch of houses in one day, met what feels like a ton of sisters. But this means, the sororities have done essentially the same thing on their end: they've met a ton of prospective members. How do they keep them all straight and know who is who?

Well, there are actually pretty complex behind-the-scenes inner workings of rush week that are planned weeks if not months in advance, and fine tuned over the years. Some sororities have a system as well organized as an operation of a fortune 500 company. It really is incredible!

For the most part, when you walk in the door and get matched up with a sister, that match was intentional. Most likely, she already knows your name and what you look like. She may even know what sports you play. Of course she may not fess up to that, and may ask you casually as if she hasn't a clue. But rest assured, you're talking to that particular sister for a specific reason. Maybe it's because she plays soccer too, and therefore it's expected that conversation will be easier because you have something in common to talk about. And later in the week, you may even get to talk with the President because either she heard great things about you and wanted to meet you in person, or because some sisters really like you while others don't, and she needed to meet you in person to be the tie-breaker.

You needn't worry too much about the behind the scenes inner workings, as long as you just do your best to be friendly, positive, and interesting (and interested), then that's really all you can do.

So let's go back to the example of how you talked to the girl on Day 1 about how you both play soccer. And during that conversation, maybe you mentioned that you love the Spanish culture and can't wait to visit South America next summer. Well then, don't be surprised if on Day 2, you are speaking to a girl from Argentina, or a sister who just visited Argentina last year. It's not a coincidence. It's a well-oiled machine.

Getting back to how the sororities make their decisions on who gets cut and who gets invited back to the next round, that's equally as complex as the match-ups.

As I mentioned, every Sorority is different, and has their own process, but I can give you a general idea of how it works from the perspective of the process behind my own Sorority's rush meetings.

After each rush event (and between rush events), each sister that got the opportunity to chat with a rushee swiftly writes down a few notes about her impression. Then, on to the next rush event that day. At the end of each day, the girls break quickly, then reconvene in one large room venue, perhaps a university classroom, completely in secret.

The Rush Chairperson and the President usually run the meeting, and they go down the list of all the girls from that day, one by one, and every sister who had an opportunity to speak with that particular girl stands up and expresses her impression of the rushee to the rest of her chapter's sisters, one at a time. Everyone listens intently to what their sister has to say, and then uses some sort of a ranking or grading chart to give the rushee a score for the day. The girls with the top scores are the ones who get invited back the following day, and the girls with the top cumulative scores at the end of Rush week are the ones who are invited to join.

As a rushee, that's why it's important to leave a really good impression with everyone you meet, not just one or two sisters. If you were friendly to one, but then not friendly to another, imagine their meeting that evening. One sister would stand up and say "Katherine was the sweetest girl, so friendly and nice, and she would be a great asset to our chapter because she's a singer and philanthropist, and she played soccer all through high school." But then the next sister would stand up and say "You know what, I had the opposite impression. She didn't smile at me or make eye contact, and I felt she was cold and didn't want to get to know me or be friendly with me." She may not even mention the face that you speak three languages and were the valedictorian, because all she cared about is that you were off-putting! Well, how do you think you'll fare on the ranking system that evening? Certainly not as well as you would have if you'd left a good impression on both sisters, so that each of them had stood up and said wonderful glowing things about you, right?

Chapter 7: What You Need to Know as a Pledge

Rule#1: Be on Time

The last thing you want is to be late for a formal rush. Don't be too early though either. As a rule of thumb 5 to 15 minutes early is good. 30 minutes is too much and just plain desperate! This rule is applicable every step of the way, even after you have been invited to pledge. The last thing you want is to make your new sisters wait on you, and possibly regret their decision to invite you to join.

Rule#2: Teamwork is Key

The group of girls that ends up joining a new Sorority at the same time is called a Pledge Class. These girls will likely become your closest friends, since you're going through the same thing at the same time, and together. Work with them as a team and show good will towards a group effort. Remember these girls will be by your side for the next 4 years!

Rule #3: Give It Your All

As a pledge class, you will be attending new events, meeting new sisters, and you may be asked to do some things that you feel are ridiculous or silly at best. Try to have a good attitude about this, and give it your all. For example, on Bid Night, we had to dress up in pretty dresses, and go sing new songs (that we didn't even fully know the words to yet) in front of each fraternity, at their front door. Given that I hate singing to begin with, this was not fun for me. But you know what? I gave it my all, and had a good, positive attitude about it, showing the girls who had just invited me into their Sorority that I can be a good sport and make a sincere effort.

Rule#4: Don't Get Wasted

Though rare these days, there have been occurrences where some sororities would waste their recruits with alcohol. Other sororities are more subtle. If you are asked if you want to drink some alcohol, say no if you can. You are there to work your way up and become a respected member of the sisterhood, not to get ridiculously drunk and make a fool of yourself. The name of the game is self control!

Rule#5: Be Easygoing and Fun Spirited

Since you are now a prospective new member of this Sorority, but still a pledge, the last thing you should do is be bossy or hard to get along with. Sometimes they may have silly games or ridiculous requirements, and you should go along with it within reason. As a general rule, embarrassing yourself is fair game. But you must avoid embarrassing others while doing so. For example, if you're told to cluck like a chicken, just do it, it's not a big deal. If you are told to share an embarrassing story, go ahead, and laugh at yourself with everyone else at the end. Generally, just be mature and fun-spirited.

On the other hand, you should never do anything scandalous, or anything that makes you or others feel uncomfortable or lower their self-esteem. Sororities want obedience and wit. So if you are told to undress in public, try to get out of it by making a joke about how no one wants to see you naked. If you are told to slap someone, ask permission to slap yourself instead. If you are told to vandalize school property, then express how you feel about the school being your home now. The bottom line is this: If a Sorority or Sorority sister tries to make you do anything that feels uncomfortable or just plain wrong, trust your instinct and get out of the situation. No person, or Sorority, is worth compromising yourself for. Being strong shows self-confidence and is an attractive quality. That will catch the attention of the right people and you will gain respect, even if you don't realize it at the moment.

Rule#6: Being in a Sorority is a Time Commitment

You'll need to understand from the beginning, being in a Sorority requires that you commit a certain amount of time and effort towards the goals of the Sorority as a whole. This is bigger than just you as an individual. You may be expected to meet the grade point average, comply with a minimum time of service, contribute on committees, and attend certain meetings and social events.

Quitting is of course an option, at any stage. However, before you quit, think carefully. A quitter will be somewhat branded for their entire stay in college. Most sororities will never accept a quitter of one Sorority as a rushee again. Last but not the least, you've made it this far, so why not see it thru to the end? Think of it as an investment and you're very near the maturity period! Sororities have lots to offer including life-long connections that you may help your career twenty-years from now. Keep this long term benefit in mind before deciding to quit.

Conclusion

Thank you again for purchasing this book!

I hope this book was able to help you better understand the experience of Sorority rush and how to make the cut! Rush and Sorority life can be a lot of fun, but there are some serious aspects too. Sororities hold their members in high regard and require each member to uphold a tradition of leadership, community service and a minimum grade point average, usually higher than a merely passing classes.

The information given in this book is not meant to scare you, it's just intended to provide information so that you know what you're getting in to and know how to plan for it. This way you will manage your expectations and perform better.

Remember, getting in is just the start of it all. You need to keep yourself in check at all times because even a Sorority member can be sanctioned or expelled. Have fun but always be responsible, reasonable, and mature.

Also, it is to your advantage not to excessively antagonize rival sororities. They're just another group similar to your Sorority, and you should treat them respectfully and if nothing else, just ignore them altogether. "If you can't say something nice, don't say anything at all," right? In most cases, you will find yourself working with them after you graduate.

Finally, if you enjoyed this book, please take the time to share your thoughts and post a review on Amazon. It'd be greatly appreciated!

Thank you and good luck!

Made in the USA
Middletown, DE
22 December 2022

20007266R00031